Teach Them While They're Young

Table of Contents

Summary 5

Chapter 1: History 7

Chapter 2: Wealth 9

Chapter 3: Love 11

Chapter 4: Manifestation 13

Chapter 5 Psychological ware fare 17

Chapter 6: Save The Future 19

Affirmations and Journaling 21

    I am loved 22

    My dreams are coming true 23

    I can do it 24

    I learn from my mistakes 27

    I act responsibly 28

    I love myself even though I sometimes fail 29

    Everyday brings new opportunities 30

    I have faith in myself 31

    I trust in my abilities 32

    I am unique 33

    I can become whatever I want to be 34

    I will embrace change 35

    I will accomplish great results 36

    I will find creative solutions to my problems 37

Summary

At a young age as parents it's important that we take the time to teach and explain to our children the knowledge of self. I had to learn everything that I currently know now later on in life. When we are less distracted we have the ability to be ahead of where we are now. That's why it's important to teach our youth by any means. As an older generation we are trying to save the future, and teach the important value of loving yourself. You cannot love anybody until you love yourself.

Chapter 1: History

The first human was an Asiatic woman born near Ethiopia and Kenya is she produced asexually (born without a man sperm no man needed to reproduce). This is before her chromosomes split (xx-xy) creating a variation or different type of woman we call man. Men are mutated females the xy chromosome is a mutation of the xx chromosome. The Moorish woman is god. If the world was to end today the woman is the only being that has the bone density to travel through the atmospheres radiation and survive and begin life on another planet. The mother, father, and child are a copy of each other called a factual start from Allah. The truth is there are no male and female. We are chemical reaction of the gonads. We are all female until 5 or 6 months, and that is when the chemical is released in the gonads that produce estrogen. There are tribes in Africa where males are born with female parts. The gonads do not become activated until the age of 12, and then they develop a penis. They know that they are male but, their (y) chromosome, and bone density is underdeveloped. We have to undo the European mindset, which; is the battle and the weapon for us to fight among each other.

Before we were called black or African American we were called Asiatic. The term black came from the government after we came out of the slavery. The term black also keeps us enslaved through the government. We aren't considered as human in the Constitution. This is

Chapter 1: History

important because you do not want the children growing up in this system not understanding the black laws. The entire system is built to destroy our race of people. Not only physically, but mentally, and spiritually.

The youth would never get a chance to know how powerful they are. They shouldn't learn this by television or Social media. It's our responsibility as parents to educate ourselves to teach them. Unfortunately, history is not taught in the homes or even in schools for the most part. Knowing our history will increase our youth's confidence. Knowing that they will have the power to manifest anything that they want or desire. They will come to realize that nothing can stop them from doing whatever they want.

We have had a lot of culture leaders come along the way over the last 100 years. All of them played a huge part in our cultures history. People like Martin Luther King Jr., Malcom X, Marcus Garvey, and the black panthers movement just to name a few. There is one Leader that has gotten lost in the history. But unless you're in tuned with the enlightening of your higher self you'll know who he is and his name is Prophet Noble Drew Ali. There are no schools that teach about him, and quite frankly they never will. Prophet Noble Drew Ali was the first person to bring Islam to the west. He was the one that introduced our birth right back to us.

The language change came which; caused division, and it conquered the world. Our spiritual system has been switched into the religious teachings of man depiction of mental warfare. You know the use of religion, fear of death, and free labor. Now we fought against slavery and oppression and it ended it with a treaty of peace

Chapter 2: Wealth

In our communities poverty is a common thing. Wealth is just something most have only seen and experienced through watching TV. A wealthy person only makes up 2% of America, and what we don't realize about wealth is that it takes generations to accumulate it. At a young age children are like sponges, and witness everything you do, so that means that they are front row witnesses of your stress, and happiness. Anything worth having taken a risk in creating, and that is a mindset that has to be developed once creating a line of generational wealth. Being on the frontline and creating wealth isn't for everybody, but someone has to do it. Nowadays everyone is on the search for ways to become self-employed. We should market to our people the fact we need a bank that buys back the resources that we have in our possessions; which means we have some educating and work to do under the radar without outside inferences. Knowledge is wealth, and I choose to take knowledge over money any day. Unfortunately, our educational system hasn't taken the time to teach our children about wealth, or creating the minds to have wealth. Wealth has to be a bloodline trait, if you think about it. The wealthiest people in the world today have blood money, meaning coming through the family line. Wealth is passed down through families, and also trauma as well. We can sit around and blame the rich, and question why we can't have wealth. But if we did that we would continue the cycle of being poor. It's our responsibility to set up a future for our children. Having a poor mindset will shut the door of wealth in front of us, and keep us bound to the mindset of being poor. You become what you think, and you have the ability to control your thoughts. This kind of mindset is learned, and that is because of what was seen, and what was birthed from genetics. The word becomes flesh when you realize, and understand that you can speak whatever into manifestation. We're genetically programed to go to school, get a job, and work hard for money. The harder you work for money the poorest you would be.

The way the rich keep the poor, poor is to never teach them what they know
— Robert Kiyosaki.

You must think ahead, every move that you make has to be beneficial to you 5 years from now. Just think about it, if we would of planned 5 years ago for today. The regrets we have today wouldn't have to be, and the decisions that were made wouldn't have been made. A part of building wealth is also understanding your value. One of the biggest issues in our communities, and reasons why we can't achieve wealth for our future generations is that we have more liabilities than assets. Assets are something you can profit from, and liabilities are something that causes debt. Here are a few ways that I found helpful in the process of increasing wealth: Save on vehicles, save shelters, and don't buy useless things. Remember you must invest in yourself, and your marketing. Venture into entrepreneurship, and invest into your education

Chapter 3: Love

As parents we should teach our children firsthand about self-love. Go within before going without, love thyself is to know thyself and understand that every living thing is attached to us as a living god. Naturally children love, hatred has to be taught. As of recently the youth suicide rate has tripled to another level. That comes from children being in depression, the lack of love and bullying.

We must teach them about their history and not their history. Tell them our history doesn't start with slavery.

By the time our children get into pre – school. They have already been bombarded with negativity. The real school starts at home. Parents nowadays don't love themselves so it's impossible to teach the children about loving themselves.

It's a war on our babies {boys & Girls}. Our boys must protect the girls. The system is doing everything to make our boys hate themselves and their skin. The media put such a negative image into the public that you'll think all we're about is crime and drugs and just negative energy. Today the youth is more advance than mankind have ever been.

Chapter 3: Love

Too many children are suffering from depression and anxiety. Teach our children how to meditate and all the benefits from it. It'll balance their stress and reduce the physical and mental stress. It'll help them focus and concentrate better as well. The average attention for a child is about 9 seconds, and it decreases by the decade. So we have to fix that by these practices.

Children must gain inner peace. : Teach 1 Save 1: Children give thanks to the ancestors and those before them. The power of saving a life is better than taking a life. You have the ability to operate with free will and begin manifesting love on this planet for the generations to come. This is the blessing

Chapter 4: Manifestation

Everything you put in the universe puts out vibrations including you. For example, we learned in physics that like energy attracts like energy, which means your mind is like a loudspeaker that emits energetic energy. We must tell our children the power they hold. You have the power to create, and your power is so strong that whatever you believe has the ability to come true. You create whatever you believe you are, your creation is your reality. You have the same power as anybody. The only difference is how you apply it to your life.

You are a master of your destiny; take control of your journey.

The energy you put out in the universe comes right back. It doesn't matter if it's positive or not. You must practice affirmations to create better outcomes of your journey. It's repetition of affirmations that leads to belief and once that belief becomes a deep conviction, things begin to happen.

The problem is the information that we have programmed in our minds. We have to train our children on these same principals. We have been set up by the system, and with that we now have to teach our children how to read, how to behave, and how to dream. When you're

Chapter 4: Manifestation

manifesting different goals in your life you must be patient because blessings need space & time to develop. Don't make it a habit telling people your next move. It'll never bloom with other people's negative energy watering the seed to your blessing. "MOVE IN SILENCE".

Affirmation examples for children:
I'm smart; I'm Blessed and I can do anything.

Watch your language! It's important for our children to understand that your thoughts become things. You want to cultivate possibility and curiosity in your child. Remember that's where manifestation begins. Words like; cannot shouldn't be used by your child. They create a negative outcome every time. Your energy attracts your experiences.

Be Grateful! Grateful people are able to appreciate the good things they have, focusing on these positive parts of life instead of excessively dwelling on the negative. If you're able to feel thankful for even the little things in life that makes you happy, you attract more of the same.

Gratitude generates a positive attitude; that in turn helps to manifest even better things.

No matter what you dream about understand that everything is attainable. Nothing is impossible to become, and no goal you have set is impossible to accomplish. Believing anything is possible doesn't mean hard work, commitment, and dedication isn't required. Those things are a required piece to you believing and knowing that you're potential is limitless. If you are able to endorse the right formula to reach your goals it will be easier to silence the critical inner voice that undermines your confidence and convince you cannot achieve your goals.

Visualizing your dreams and goals is the process through the law of attraction which; is one of the most important elements. Imagine your goals or dreams in a vivid picture with detail. Seeing positive things in this way helps you to believe that you really can cultivate the life you crave.

Embrace your uniqueness, once you accept and celebrate the parts of yourself that set you apart from others. That process not only will help you reach your full potential, it will also allow you to help others reach their full potential as well. That will allow you to have self – esteem, which in turn makes it easier to attract the things you deserve.

Chapter 5: Psychological ware fare

It's our duty as parents to teach the children to be critical thinkers. So they won't become a victim of many lies being told daily. The oppressors have the agenda to attack our children as soon as they get out of the womb. The common forms of attacks we have seen is medical, and the school system. All this information must be taught in our household, before the system gets them. First thing we think, is sending our children to their system to get an education to work in their industry is the answer.

Let me make this perfectly clear. The school system was design for us to become workers not owners or controllers. John D. Rockefeller invented the school system. If you know anything about him or his family then you'll realize that it wasn't created to help our children. This is the same family that is responsible for most of the pharmaceutical companies that has been killing our elders for decades. Their plan was to control economics and all the resources in order for them to gain control and access to our children and their children.

Some of the problems with the school systems are the following: they are created to kill your creativity, and dumb you down to become a worker.

John D. Rockefeller said, "*He wants to create a nation full of workers.*"

Chapter 5: Psychological ware fare

I understand we all are not able to homeschool our children, because of the lack of economics and working hours. Think about this, the way the system is designed gives parents the disadvantage, because they will have to work all day and have no time for their children. Let's be realistic here. You come home from the job that you may hate, and a job that causes you to be too tired to even engage with your child. The workforce unfortunately has you too tired and worn out because of the labor that is required from you is much more than the wages they are paying you.

This ultimately creates a cycle that keeps on down the family line. We are basically putting our children in even worse circumstances when they reach our age.

To colonize the people's mind, you must first demonize their culture and their traditions. Once you come to understand that God is in you. You will no longer need a book to tell you how to live. Mental slavery is the worse form of slavery, because it gives you the illusion of freedom, makes you trust, love, and offend the enemy.

Chapter 6: Save The Future

Protect our children by any means necessary. The reason why I wrote this book was because I wanted to bring some awareness on some issues that we seem to keep ignoring for generations. To inform parents that it's a war on our next generation. We have two choices: Take action and save the children, or sit here and allow them to take our children's minds and souls.

Toxic masculinity is in full effect. Here are some statistics for you: 43% of boys raised by single mothers, 78% of teachers are females, and 50% of boys have about 100% feminine influence at home and school.

Toxic masculinity isn't the problem the lack of masculinity is.

The school system is failing our children, and most of us are aware of this. We have been complaining about the system for a long time. Are we going to still send our children to school? Knowing that it will continue to kill their confidence when they don't make an A on the enemy test. Stop forcing our children to go to college and come out with a hundred thousand dollars in student loans and bad credit. We set them up to fail before they left home. College was design to keep you in debt.

Chapter 6: Save The Future

Let's create wealth for the next generations, and that starts by educating ourselves on economics. Living in poverty should've been motivation enough to not let your children ever experience that feeling. For generations we have been taught the same thing. Go to school and get a job. So let's take a look around in your family. Everybody that did that is now old and still paying off his or her homes. Old age, and broken down because they been working so long. The job broke their body down.

The violence has to stop if we're going to aim to rebuild for the future. We have to understand and over stand that we are not each other's enemy. That's such a real statement, because we get so stressed and angry at our living conditions. We take it out on each other instead of the enemy.

A.I "Artificial Intelligence" is moving in as of today. Once it's welcomed by the entire country middle class will be jobless. Average citizens think going into a high-end profession will keep them safe from a situation like this. Doctors & Lawyers will also be affected by the A.I paradigm. They have the Robot Lawyers already created. I know you are wondering why is this important? And how does this affect me? Once this is effective, there will be no more jobs for the average person. You better do whatever you can right now to get ahead of this.

We must create our own products and sale, take control of our own resources, and become more economically smart.

Affirmations and Journaling

Affirmations and Journaling

I am loved

My dreams are coming true

Affirmations and Journaling

I can do it

I am intelligent

Affirmations and Journaling

I learn from my mistakes

Affirmations and Journaling

I act responsibly

I love myself even though I sometimes fail

Affirmations and Journaling

Everyday brings new opportunities

I have faith in myself

I trust in my abilities

I am unique

Affirmations and Journaling

I can become whatever I want to be

I will embrace change

I will accomplish great results

I will find creative solutions to my problems

www.ingramcontent.com/pod-product-compliance
Lightning Source LLC
Chambersburg PA
CBHW022111160426
43198CB00008B/432